IMAGES
of America

CODY

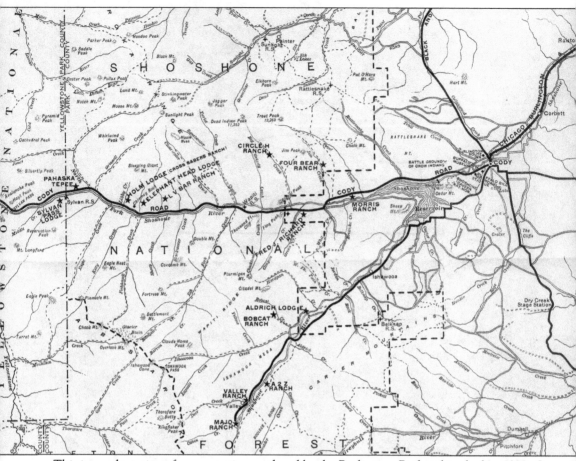

This is an adaptation of a map section produced by the Burlington Railroad in the late 1920s. It shows Cody and the regions known locally as the North Fork and the Southfork. Included are some of the ranches in both areas, the Buffalo Bill Dam and Reservoir, and the Cody Road to Yellowstone National Park. (PCA, LC96-45.11.)

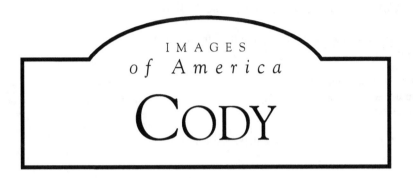

IMAGES

of America

CODY

Lynn Johnson Houze

ARCADIA
PUBLISHING

Published by Arcadia Publishing
Charleston, South Carolina

Library of Congress Catalog Card Number: 2007934178

For all general information contact Arcadia Publishing at:
Telephone 843-853-2070
Fax 843-853-0044
E-mail sales@arcadiapublishing.com
For customer service and orders:
Toll-Free 1-888-313-2665

Visit us on the Internet at www.arcadiapublishing.com

*To the memory of my parents, who instilled in me a love of history,
and to my children and my grandchildren, whom I hope will
continue to love it, too.*

CONTENTS

ACKNOWLEDGMENTS

I am fortunate to have had the support of many people in writing this book. First and foremost is Ester Johansson-Murray, local Cody historian, who encouraged me and who graciously corrected my misconceptions and my errors. I truly appreciate her help and her friendship. Bob Landgren not only let me have my choice of photographs from his mother's album, but also filled in various historic gaps in my knowledge of the power plant, the irrigation system, and anything else whenever I asked. Many thanks to the registration and the photography department staff of the Buffalo Bill Historical Center (BBHC); they have been wonderful to work with, as have Marylin Schultz and Rhonda Spaulding at the Park County Archives. The staff of the McCracken Research Library at the BBHC, Cindy Brown at the Wyoming State Archives in Cheyenne, and Leslie Waggener at the American Heritage Center at the University of Wyoming, Laramie, were patient with me in my quest to find photographs that had not been published previously. Lora Norland at the Shoshone Irrigation District Archives in Powell scanned and rescanned photographs for me, and Chris Gimmeson at the BBHC taught me a great deal about scanning images, which I really appreciate. I also want to thank Marion Pierce, Janet Dutton, Nancy and Dave Wulfing, Anne Hayes, Len Pearson, Fran Swope, and Jeremy Johnston for allowing me to use treasured family photographs, many of which have not been published previously.

I also want to thank the Wyoming State Historical Society for awarding me a Lola Homsher Grant to help with my expenses. Their financial assistance is greatly appreciated.

Finally, I would like to thank those local authors who preceded me for all the work they have done over the years in recording the history of Cody. A special thank-you to two of them: Beryl Churchill for her work dealing with the Buffalo Bill Dam and the irrigation systems and Ester Johansson-Murray for her book on the North Fork. Their books were invaluable to me.

In the interest of brevity, abbreviations will be used for the following three photograph sources in the credit lines:

Buffalo Bill Historical Center, Cody, Wyoming	BBHC
Park County Archives, Cody, Wyoming	PCA
Shoshone Irrigation District Archives, Powell, Wyoming	SIDA

INTRODUCTION

This area of northwest Wyoming, east of Yellowstone National Park, is known as the Big Horn Basin and was restricted from white settlement by treaties with the Indians in 1868. Ten years later, those restrictions were lifted and early settlers slowly began to enter the basin. By 1890, Wyoming had achieved statehood, attracting even more people.

William F. "Buffalo Bill" Cody, was visiting Sheridan, Wyoming, in 1894, when his son-in-law Horace Boal gave him a close look at this area from the top of the Big Horn Mountains, located on the eastern side of the basin. A group of Sheridan businessmen were already interested in founding a town here, and Buffalo Bill eagerly joined the effort. He saw the beauty of the region, its proximity to Yellowstone National Park (which was already attracting tourists), the abundance of game and fish, and the available land for ranching and farming. The only major thing missing was sufficient water to enable ranchers and farmers to make a living, as this is high desert country. The Shoshone River did run through the area, however, which meant there was potential for bringing more water to the land. By 1895, the Shoshone Land and Irrigation Company was formed and made up of George T. Beck, William F. Cody, Nate Salsbury, Harry Gerrans, Bronson Rumsey, Horace Alger, and George Bleistein. That year, an initial town site was laid out near DeMaris Hot Springs, two miles west of present-day Cody. Beck did not like the location or the fact that a great deal of the land was already owned by Charles DeMaris, for whom the hot springs are named, and began looking at other possibilities to the east. With that in mind, in the fall of 1895, work began on building the Cody Canal, which would carry water from the Southfork of the Shoshone River east to the town. In May 1896, Beck and surveyor Charles Hayden laid out the town at its present location.

"The Colonel," as the townspeople usually referred to him in those early years, invested a great deal of money in the birth of the town. George Beck was the town founder who lived here and oversaw its ups and downs. The Burlington Railroad, headquartered in Lincoln, Nebraska, was interested in building a spur line to Cody from Toluca, Montana, which was on the line running from Billings, Montana, to southern Wyoming. To make sure that Cody did become the terminus of the line, the Shoshone Land and Irrigation Company sold the majority of the town lots to the railroad company and dropped "Land" from their company name. An attempt at publishing a newspaper called the *Shoshone Valley News* was made in 1896, but it only lasted a short while. The first edition of the *Cody Enterprise* was published in 1899 and is still publishing today. It did go through several name changes over the years, but to this day, the masthead honors Buffalo Bill as its founder. The town of Cody was incorporated in 1901, the same year the Chicago, Burlington, and Quincy Railroad arrived on the north side of the river.

Before Cody's founding in 1896, the community of Marquette was already established near the confluence of the south and north branches of the Shoshone River, located west of the canyon formed by the river between two mountains, Rattlesnake and Cedar. It had a general store, a school, a saloon, and a number of ranches. The confluence is about eight miles west of the town of Cody and was seen as the logical place to construct a dam, thereby creating a reservoir to supply water to the western part of the Big Horn Basin. In 1902, the Newlands Reclamation Act decreed that all funds received by the federal government from the disposition and sale of public lands in the 16 Western states were to be used to construct dam and irrigation systems that were too large and too costly to be undertaken by the private sector. The Shoshone River Valley Project was the first project undertaken after the passage of this act. Cody assigned his water rights to the Reclamation Service in 1904, and work began on building and improving the road between Cody and the dam site that spring. The construction of the dam meant that the area known as Marquette would be flooded, necessitating either the removal or the abandonment of the ranches and the buildings there. This pictorial history of Cody begins with Marquette.

One

MARQUETTE AND BUFFALO BILL'S DAM

This view looks northwest of the confluence of the Southfork and the North Fork of the Shoshone River, west of Shoshone Canyon. This is the western tip of land where the community of Marquette was located before the dam was built and the Shoshone River subsequently flooded the area of 10.5 square miles. (SIDA.)

The confluence of the two branches of the river is shown from the northeast, looking toward the Southfork of the Shoshone River. The Reclamation Service photographed all ranches and land that would be underwater once the dam was completed. This photographic survey continued throughout the duration of the road work and the dam construction. (SIDA.)

A road existed on the north side of the river, which went partway into Shoshone Canyon. In the spring of 1904, work began on improving the road and extending it to the dam site. The camp seen in the distance is the lower camp, about two miles from the dam site, one of two camps that housed workers, engineers, geologists, and some families. (Wyoming State Archives, State Parks and Cultural Resources.)

10

Here the rock men are working in a very steep area of the canyon. The rock is granite, but the work was done with picks, shovels, and sledgehammers. The hours were long and the work difficult and dangerous. The eight-mile dirt road that began at the Cody railroad depot was only a single lane and not very wide by today's standards. (SIDA.)

The westernmost tunnel of the two was just east of the dam site sits at the foot of the hill. The narrowness of these tunnels became more of a traffic hazard in later years as vehicles increased in size and were capable of traveling faster speeds. Five unidentified workers stand among the rocks on the south side of the river. (American Heritage Center, University of Wyoming.)

The three tunnels are visible here close together. A great deal of blasting was done to begin the tunnels, but the workers chipped away at the rock with hand tools to finish them. The road and tunnels took just over a year to complete as they were usable in July 1905. (PCA, 99-37-140.)

Freight wagons being pulled by sure-footed mules are bringing construction materials and supplies to the dam site. In wintertime, when the narrow road was covered with snow and ice, the trip was extremely dangerous and accidents happened all too often. (PCA, 95-62-25.)

This bridge over the North Fork of the Shoshone River connects Tom Trimmer's ranch at Marquette with the Cody Road to Yellowstone. The road is known by various names including North Fork Highway, the Cody Road, or Yellowstone Highway. The Trimmer ranch was one of the properties flooded by the creation of the new reservoir. (SIDA.)

George Marquette came to this area of the Big Horn Basin in 1878. He settled first near the town of Meeteetse, south of Cody. He then built a home with an attached saloon on the Southfork and gave his name to the area. He was the first postmaster of the Marquette Post Office from April 1891 to 1899. Known affectionately as "Uncle George," he was an outstanding fiddle player, playing for dances held at his saloon. (PCA, 86-02-063.)

Payne and MacGlashan's General Store was one of only a few buildings in the community of Marquette. Additionally, a post office, a school, and a saloon provided services to the ranch owners in the 10.5-square-mile area. They were also the social center of the community. (PCA, 00-6-273.)

Pictured here about 1898 is Marquette School No. 1, located on the Howard Brundage ranch, with the students, the teacher, and some guests present. The school was moved before the reservoir flooded the area. Teacher Dolly Martin is the first person standing on the left in the second row. She later taught at Marquette No. 2 and Marquette No. 3 schools. (Nancy Trimmer Wulfing collection.)

In 1905, Marquette held a Frontier Day rodeo near Payne and MacGlashan's General Store. Broncho—as it was spelled then—busting was a favorite event. Rodeos began in the late 1880s and were a way for cowboys to test their skills against their friends and their neighbors. These early rodeos were very basic with no corrals to separate the contestants from the audience. (BBHC, P.69.1196.)

Buffalo Bill's Buffalo Meadow Ranch was in the Marquette area, located east of Sheep Mountain. Buffalo Bill received $3,900 from the federal government for the 80 acres that composed his ranch. He is seated in the buggy on the right with his very good friend Dr. Frank "White Beaver" Powell. The other people are unidentified. (BBHC, P.69.1919.)

This is the Thomas Trimmer homestead as it appeared on November 12, 1908. Trimmer settled here in 1886 on 600 acres. In 1900, he married Marquette schoolteacher Dolly Martin. The federal government paid widow Dolly $12,000 for their entire ranch. When Marquette was flooded, she and son Tommy moved into town. (SIDA.)

This is the Logan Ranch with the Southfork of the Shoshone River and Sheep Mountain behind it. The photograph was taken on December 11, 1908, more than a year before the ranchers moved away. The horse and buggy used by the Reclamation Service to travel from ranch to ranch can be seen in the center foreground. (SIDA.)

The wooden forms were built first, one linear section at a time. Rocks weighing between 20 and 50 pounds each were placed within the frame, and concrete was poured over them. The length of the dam from one side of the river to the other is 200 feet. (PCA, 00-06-249.)

By mid-November 1908, the top of the Shoshone Dam was 15 feet above the original low water level. Precautions were taken to prevent the concrete from freezing by heating it and covering it. Frozen concrete must be replaced as it has weakened. (SIDA.)

The last bucket of concrete was poured at 11:00 a.m. on January 15, 1910, when the temperature was -15 degrees Fahrenheit and almost six years after work began on the road. Daniel Webster Cole, chief constructing engineer, is standing to the right of the worker whose hand is on the bucket. Carl Johansson, a local Cody worker, is standing second from left, wearing a cap and with his legs crossed. (PCA, 00-06-274.)

Shoshone Dam is 325 feet high and was the tallest dam in the world upon completion. The spring runoff in 1910 began to fill the reservoir, and by late October it was full. The water from the reservoir is used by towns to the east of Cody in the Big Horn Basin. Cody receives its water from the Southfork of the Shoshone River. (Wyoming State Archives, State Parks and Cultural Resources.)

The dam's spillway is used to control the water level in the reservoir. In 1990, when construction was begun to add 25 feet to the height of the dam, control gates were installed for better regulation of the water levels. It was finished three years later. (Wyoming State Archives, State Parks and Cultural Resources.)

The confluence of the two branches of the Shoshone River looked like this in January 1913, when the water was drained from the reservoir to make repairs to the dam. If any structures had been left prior to the original filling of the reservoir in 1910, they had disappeared by the time this photograph was taken. A geyser is on the land that juts out between the two forks. (BBHC, Jack Richard Collection, P.89.88.)

Shoshone Canyon
Cody-Road
Wed. Frost Photo

This is a bird's-eye view of the Cody Road heading west through Shoshone Canyon to the dam in the background. Notice the cars waiting to go through the tunnel on the lower right side. The traffic on the way down the "Dam Hill" had the right of way, and horn honking alerted the drivers to approaching vehicles. There were several spots that were a little wider where a car could pull off to allow the downhill car to come through. The road was widened in several spots in the 1920s, which made travel a little easier, but there are still Cody residents who have interesting stories to tell of learning to drive, especially the shifting process, on this hill. (Vaun Landgren collection.)

This is the Shoshone Reservoir as it looked in the 1920s. The view is from the dam looking west toward the main part of the lake or reservoir. In addition to providing water for farmers, ranchers, and homeowners, the lake provides recreational activities for area residents. Boating, sailing, and fishing have always been popular. In recent years, the lake and the winds that come across it have attracted windsurfers from around the country. (Vaun Landgren collection.)

On April 28, 1959, a fire broke out in a toolshed and workshop at the top of the dam. A spark from a welding torch ignited a gasoline-soaked outboard motor, and attempts to use a fire extinguisher were unsuccessful. The high winds soon had the building in total flames, which took two hours to put out. The fire resulted in a loss of $10,000 in equipment. (PCA, 02-38-15.)

A rock slide occurred June 19, 1959, at 3:00 p.m., closing the road. As a result, three new longer tunnels were constructed, which offered protection to vehicles from future slides, and a bridge and the roadbed were improved. The entire project took almost two years to complete. On February 26, 1946, the 100th birthday of William F. "Buffalo Bill" Cody, both the dam and the reservoir were renamed in his honor. They are now known as the Buffalo Bill Dam and the Buffalo Bill Reservoir. (PCA, 99-37-151.)

Two

EARLY BEGINNINGS

This is one of the earliest known photographs of a house in what would become the town of Cody. It was taken in 1888 or 1889 when there were only a few scattered homesteads in this area. These early pioneers not only settled before Cody was founded, but also predate Wyoming statehood, in 1890. (BBHC, P.5.1594.)

A. C. Newton bought the Trail Creek homestead in 1893 from Frenchman Paul Breteche. The original homesteaders were partners Vic Arland and Jim Corbett, who both came in 1880. They established a trading post alongside an Indian trail at the base of Rattlesnake Mountain, a few miles northwest of present-day Cody. A. C. Newton was the first member of several Newton families who came from Illinois. (BBHC, P.5.1428.)

This view looking west toward Cedar Mountain on the left and Rattlesnake on the right shows how barren the town site of Cody was in the mid-1890s. Some wooden structures had been built, but tents are still in evidence. With an elevation of 5,000 feet and a high desert climate, irrigation was an absolute necessity for ranching, farming, and survival. (BBHC, P.5.1454A.)

Work on building the Cody Canal, which would bring water from the Southfork to the town of Cody, began in the fall of 1895. The men worked long, hard hours and were paid about $1 per day. Most of them were immigrants who stayed in Cody only until the canal was finished. In the background is part of the flume that would carry the water to the residents. (PCA, 86-033-012.)

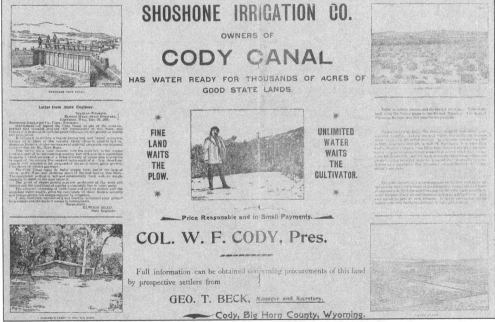

This Shoshone Irrigation Company advertisement appeared in the *Cody Enterprise* on September 28, 1899. It was premature, as the canal was not yet ready—nor would it be for several years. The company was composed of town founders William F. "Buffalo Bill" Cody, George T. Beck (manager), Nate Salsbury (Buffalo Bill's Wild West business manager), Horace Alger, Bronson Rumsey, Harry Gerrans, and George Bleistein. (BBHC, MS6, Series I).

The Cody Canal came from the Southfork, around Cedar Mountain, and to the east toward Cody. Vaun Landgren is standing on a section of the flume that went over Sulphur Creek, located just west of Cody. The creek begins southeast of Cody and runs to the north into the Shoshone River, where it ends. (Vaun Landgren collection.)

Stan Landgren, husband of Vaun Landgren, stands on the edge of Sulphur Creek, named for the high presence of that gas in it and in the nearby Shoshone River. The Crow Indians had named it the Stinking Water River, and for many years after whites came to the area, the two names were used interchangeably. (Vaun Landgren collection.)

This road runs west from Cody through Shoshone Canyon to the dam and crosses Sulphur Creek on its way out of town. Rather than the bridge going straight across at the same height as the road, the road actually went down to the bridge and then back up again on the other side. (PCA, 95-18-168.)

A little farther west of the Sulphur Creek Bridge is an area known as Colter's Hell. When John Colter came through this area in 1807–1808, he reported seeing a great deal of geyser activity. Many didn't believe him, but he was correct. This particular crater is located approximately five-and-a-half miles northwest of the town. (SIDA.)

Cody was founded in May 1896, when the streets were laid out by George Beck and surveyor Charles Hayden. This house, built by Jerry Ryan on Alger Avenue, is one of the earliest permanent structures. Beck, manager of the Shoshone Irrigation Company, asked Ryan to attach a proper schoolroom to his house to replace the various temporary quarters, such as the back room of Primm's Saloon. (PCA, 00-06-31.)

Buffalo Bill realized the importance of a newspaper to a new town. In August 1899, he brought a Babcock printing press from Duluth, Minnesota, where his sister Helen Wetmore and her husband, Hugh, used it to print the *Duluth Free Press*. Col. J. H. Peake, a newspaperman from Washington, D.C., arrived to be the editor. Anna "Granny" Peake, who ran the paper after her husband died in 1905, is the woman shown here. (PCA, 00-06-46.)

28

Wide streets were standard in Cody at the insistence of George T. Beck. His reasoning was that fires could not spread as rapidly or as far if the streets were wide, and this proved to be accurate. An additional benefit was that wagons and coaches had more room to maneuver and to turn around. This photograph was taken about 1899. (American Heritage Center, University of Wyoming.)

This house was built on the corner of Alger Avenue and Seventeenth Street, also known as the "Greybull Hill" because it leads to the town of Greybull. The photograph was taken in the fall of 1902 and shows that the area is still sparsely settled. The Bargain Box, a resale clothing and miscellaneous goods shop run by Christ Episcopal Church, occupies the updated house today. (BBHC, P.5.1598.)

L. E. WEBSTER,
PHOTO
CODY, WYO,

CODY. WYO.,

Cody was almost 10 years old at the time of this photograph. The Irma Hotel is the two-story building in the center of the photograph at the western edge of town. Churches have been built by the Episcopalians, the Methodists, and the Presbyterians, but saloons still outnumber them. The "Little Red School" opened in 1904 but was quickly outgrown, so an addition was put on several

V. 21ST 1905.

years later. The main streets running east and west are named after the town fathers, except for the main street, named after Gen. Philip Sheridan. The north-south streets use numbers, such as Second, Third, and so on. The *Cody Enterprise* reported that $200,000 was spent on improvements and new construction in 1905. (Marion Pierce collection.)

671~ Building a home on the Shoshone Project Along the Cody branch of the CB&Q. WUL Dec. 15 1908

The Chicago, Burlington, and Quincy Railroad (called the CB&Q or just Burlington locally) built a spur line to Cody—seen here—from the Toluca, Montana, station on the north-south line connecting Billings, Montana, to southern Wyoming. Service began in November 1901, increasing both the number of tourists and settlers coming to Cody. (SIDA.)

This bridge over the Shoshone River connects the town, on the left, to the railroad depot north of the river. It replaces the original pedestrian bridge, though horses could be walked over it. The railroad's arrival created the need for a larger and stronger bridge. Visible in the background on the right is the first road to the Shoshone Dam. (American Heritage Center, University of Wyoming.)

E. M. Westerveld, of the Land and Industrial Commission for the CB&Q Railroad, stands near the westernmost end of the track. The depot and the water tank can be seen in the distance. On the right is the Cody Burlington Inn, a hotel built by the railroad in the early 1920s. (Wyoming State Archives, State Parks and Cultural Resources.)

This is a typical scene at the Cody Depot when the train was expected. Coaches and wagons met the tourists and took them to hotels for the first night. The next morning, they left for sightseeing in Yellowstone National Park, or perhaps to go hunting. (Wyoming State Archives, State Parks and Cultural Resources.)

The Irma Hotel, which cost $80,000 to build, had a grand opening on November 18, 1902. Buffalo Bill named the hotel after his youngest daughter, whose engagement to Lt. Clarence Stott was announced that evening. There were at least 500 people who attended the gala event, more than the population of Cody. Jakie Schwoob, manager of the Cody Trading Company, is standing in front of the Irma when it was still quite new. (Len Pearson collection.)

The Irma soon became the social center of the town. During one of the Colonel's trips home, he is seen standing with his arm raised beneath a 1904 campaign banner advocating Theodore Roosevelt for president, Fennimore Chatterton for governor of Wyoming, and M. S. Ridgely for state senator. (Wyoming State Archives, State Parks and Cultural Resources.)

This is one of the coaches that carried passengers between the depot and the hotels, including the Irma. In these early years, the main street of town was not Sheridan Avenue but Fourth Street, now Twelfth Street, which ran north-south along the east side of the Irma. This street connected directly to the Depot Bridge, also known as the Twelfth Street Bridge. (Wyoming State Archives, State Parks and Cultural Resources.)

A group of dudes from the Howard Eaton ranch in Sheridan, Wyoming, came through Cody on their way to Yellowstone in 1906. They are stretched across Thirteenth Street between Beck and Alger Avenues. The Hart Mountain Inn, owned by "Badland" Dave and Aurilla McFall and a favorite of many visitors, is to the right. The Darrah Lumber building still exists in 2007. (Wyoming State Archives, State Parks and Cultural Resources.)

When ranchers and farmers came to town for their supplies, many would board their horses at the Keystone Barn and stay across the street at the Hart Mountain Inn to the east. Barely visible on the front of the barn is a billboard announcing the visit of Buffalo Bill's Wild West to Billings, Montana, the closest to Cody that the Wild West appeared. Cody Auditorium occupies this site today. (PCA, 95-18-142.)

Brundage Hardware Company was one of the first buildings on the north side of Sheridan Avenue between Eleventh and Twelfth Streets. Built in 1898 by Howard Brundage, it housed a business owned by Richard Roth in the other half, and the stores shared a common wall. Brundage Hardware also had a shooting range in the basement. (PCA, 86–024-040.)

The Cody Volunteer Fire Department Hook and Ladder Company No. 1 is seen in front of the original fire hall located on Salsbury Avenue. Some of the firefighters in this photograph are Dr. James Bradbury, Guss Holm, George Taylor, Andy Larson, Barney Cone, Walter Schwoob, Archie Abbott, Roy McGinnis, Carl Hammitt, Col. J. H. Peake, and Nick Noble. (PCA, 88-07-002.)

By 1909, the Cody Volunteer Fire Department had been outfitted with slickers and helmets by Buffalo Bill. Additional equipment, such as hose carts, had also been acquired, but fighting fires was difficult when the only water supply came from ditches and the canal. A fire alarm call box can be seen in the foreground. (PCA, 99-37-06.)

One of the first three-story homes in Cody, the Nearby Ranch was "out-of-town" when it was built in 1904 by Frank and Darlene Newton Ingraham. This view looking toward the east shows the sparsely settled plains just a year later. Darlene is the sister of A. C. Newton, owner of Trail Creek Ranch, whom her family visited in 1901. (SIDA.)

This view of Cody looks west toward Rattlesnake Mountain with the Irma Hotel in the distance and the Nearby Ranch in the foreground. A water tower sits on the top of the bench between Twelfth and Thirteenth Streets (left). The Cody Canal comes along the base of the hill and curls around the homes to the Nearby Ranch, exiting at the bottom center of the photograph. (PCA, 95-60.32.)

The construction of the Masonic Temple on Twelfth Street began in 1912. The Masons are measuring the cornerstone in preparation for installing it in the front right-hand corner of the building during a special ceremony. William F. Cody was a member of the Scottish Rite Masons and donated money to help fund the new building. (PCA, 00-06.65.)

During the construction of the Masonic Temple, one of Cody's notorious winds, a "Cody Zephyr," blew down sections of several walls. Here they have been rebuilt, but the cornerstone has not been replaced yet, nor has the ledge over the front door been repaired. Because of the wind destruction, the building was not finished until 1915. (PCA, 95-62.60.)

Freight wagons are lined up on Thirteenth Street, facing north, and appear to be hauling bags of wool, as there are many sheep ranches around Cody. Four-horse teams were standard, but heavier wagonloads required larger teams, such as those hitched to the first wagon. Before the arrival of the train, freight came by wagon so it was common to see 8-horse and 10-horse teams. (PCA, 95-62-54.)

Cody had quickly become a popular place to visit as many new residents invited family and friends to see their new town. Dorothy Newton, daughter of A. C. Newton, and three friends from the East, are out for a horseback ride along with Happy, the dog. Dorothy is the second rider from the left. (BBHC, P.69.2011.)

With the beginning of train service to Cody in 1901, tourism increased. After spending the first night in Cody, tourists traveled by horse-drawn coaches 36 miles to Wapiti Inn for their second night before continuing on to Pahaska Tepee at the East Entrance of Yellowstone National Park the next day. When cars replaced wagons, Wapiti Inn became a lunch stop. (BBHC, P.6.644.)

The area around Cody was known to be rich in oil, gas, and minerals, and in 1911, oil was discovered in Oregon Basin, southeast of Cody. The Cody Oil and Development Company, whose shareholders included town founders Cody, Gerrans, Beck, Bleistein, and Rumsey, began drilling there. Beck is third from the left and Cody is fourth from the right. The others are unidentified. (BBHC, P.69.1048.)

The Southfork area, located southwest of Cody, had been attracting settlers as early as the 1880s. Seen here is a volcanic plug named Castle Rock, located approximately 20 miles from the town. It is also known as Colter Rock because it is thought that John Colter passed by it in 1807–1808. (Len Pearson collection.)

These young girls are at a party held at an unidentified Southfork home. The girls are all dressed up in their Sunday best. Included in the first row are Ina McCleary Moore (standing next to the stove), Joan Reener (third from the right), and Loma Stevens (fifth from the right). Others present include Anna Blood, Jessie ?, Gladys ?, and Mary ?. (PCA, 87-12-002.)

The Cody Trading Company moved to this location at the corner of Sheridan Avenue and Thirteenth Street in 1898. Jakie Schwoob came from Buffalo, New York, to manage it and by 1920 owned it outright. The store carried food, clothes, and everything imaginable for the time. A fire in 1913 burned the entire building, but Schwoob rebuilt it on the same site just a year later. (American Heritage Center, University of Wyoming.)

For a year or so, the Cody Trading Company occupied the former Iowa Store located across the street to the north and west of the burned-out store. When the store reopened, it was bigger and better than ever. This is the graniteware department, which sold enameled iron utensils and pots that were speckled and looked as though they were made from granite. (PCA, 86-024-002.)

R. C. Shultz was the proprietor of Western Drug, one of the earliest drugstores in town, located on the north side of Sheridan Avenue between Twelfth and Thirteenth Streets. Western Drug carried a line of Kodak camera equipment and supplies, some of which can be seen behind Shultz. Frequently he would enter a float in the Fourth of July parade to promote Kodak and their line of photographic equipment. (PCA, 95-62.8.)

Carl Hammitt was city marshal of Cody from late 1902 until 1938. This was a part-time job as he also worked in construction. Additionally, he was a volunteer fireman and is in the photograph of the men taken in front of the fire hall. His brother Frank Hammitt died in 1904 under mysterious circumstances in the area north of Cody known as the Sunlight-Crandall area. (PCA, 86-033-01.)

Three

OUTFITTERS, GUIDES, AND RANCHES

The Mahlon Frost family arrived in the Big Horn Basin from the Midwest in 1885, first settling on the Southfork near Valley Ranch before moving to the Sage Creek area east of Carter Mountain. Mahlon's sons Ned (left) and Jesse, with his son Jack, evidently had a great day fishing in late 1903. Ned became a well-known outfitter throughout the region. (BBHC, P.69.1403.)

Jim McLaughlin, hunter and trapper, homesteaded in a valley in the upper Southfork region located 43 miles from Cody. He named his place the Mountain Home Ranch. According to the phrase written on this photograph, his alias was the "Great Rocky Mountain Goat Shooter." However, he was probably hunting mountain sheep as there were no mountain goats in this area then. (PCA, 86-033-009.)

The great Rocky Mountain Goat Shooter, alias Jim McLaughlin Mountain Home Ranch, Valley, Wyo. 1891

By 1906, McLaughlin's ranch looked like this. It was renamed Valley Ranch by the next owners, I. H. "Larry" Larom and Winthrop "Win" Brooks, who bought it in 1915. It was a dude ranch in the summer and a boy's preparatory school during the year until the middle of the Depression. Larom bought out Brooks, of the Brooks Brothers store in New York City, in 1926. (BBHC, P.5.1591.)

Another early ranch on the Southfork was the Majo Ranch, shown here in 1904–1905. It was started by hunting guide John "Reckless" Davis, a very good friend of Buffalo Bill's and a guide on his hunting trips. Unfortunately, at the age of 50, Davis died of ptomaine poisoning after eating canned vegetables while visiting Pahaska Tepee, Buffalo Bill's hunting lodge on the North Fork. (PCA, 00-06-126.)

This fur trader's cabin is located on Trail Creek Ranch and was probably built by Vic Arland and John Corbett. They left here in 1883, moving 10 miles southeast to Cottonwood Creek near the Shoshone River, where they set up a trading post on the Billings-Lander Trail. By the early 1950s, the cabin had fallen into disrepair. (BBHC, P.5.1595.)

W. F. Cody wrote on this photograph, "The life I love. Camp head of Shoshone river Wyo. Nov. 20th 1901." The hunters included many of his old friends such as Iron Tail, Black Fox, William Sweeney, Dr. Frank "White Beaver" Powell, the Reverend George Beecher, Mike Russell, and official photographer Ed Robinson. Artist Irving Bacon later commemorated this trip with an oil painting based on this photograph. (BBHC, P.69.977.)

This is the North Fork hunting camp of P. B. Wells and Johnny Goff, local hunting guides. Goff (right) led hunts throughout the Rocky Mountain region, including a famous Colorado hunt with Theodore Roosevelt. The other man may be Wells as he was on both the 1905 Roosevelt hunt and a Yellowstone National Park hunt in 1906, the same year this photograph was taken. (Jeremy Johnston collection.)

One Day's Hunt with Frost and Richards, Cody, Wyo.

Two of the most well-known and well-respected outfitters and guides in this region were Ned Frost (left) and Fred Richard (center). Shortly after meeting in the early 1900s, they became friends and informal business partners. They were among the first guides to charge hunters for their guiding services and often guided celebrities, including the Prince of Monaco in 1913. (Wyoming State Archives, State Parks and Cultural Resources.)

Ned Frost and Fred Richard bought the Grinder Ranch on the North Fork, halfway between Cody and Yellowstone, in 1910 and soon were guiding dudes and hunters alike. On some trips, there were as many as 150 tourists. A little over five years later, they sold the tourist part of the business to concentrate on ranching, guiding hunts, and summer fishing trips. Their ranch was torn down in 1999. (PCA, 95-62-59.)

Col. W. F. Cody enjoyed returning to Cody at the end of each season of Buffalo Bill's Wild West for relaxation and hunting, bringing friends from the Wild West and others from around the country with him. This was the 1904 hunting party in front of the Irma, led by Buffalo Bill (center). His nephew Walter F. Goodman is on the white horse next to him. (Wyoming State Archives, State Parks and Cultural Resources.)

Winter was always a challenging time for guides and hunters in this area, but Benny Reif (left) and Verne Spencer seem to be enjoying the snow and the cold. Young Cody native Spencer was friends with Buffalo Bill and later guided many celebrities, including Ernest Hemingway, Wallace Beery, Herbert Hoover, Spencer Tracy, Clark Gable, and Carole Lombard. (American Heritage Center, University of Wyoming.)

Tex Thomas owned the White Horse Stage Line, which carried passengers between the Cody Depot and the local hotels. He may have taken tourists on short day trips but the carriage pictured is not suited for trips into Yellowstone as there is no protection from wind and storms. Other coaches had roofs and canvas sides that could be rolled down when the weather turned poor. (PCA, 80-12-178.)

Snowballing in July on Cody Road to Park with Nordquist and James.

Tourists traveling to Yellowstone have to be prepared for all sorts of weather. Pete Nordquist and ? James were guiding this group to Yellowstone along the Cody Road in July when a snowball fight broke out. This trip may have occurred prior to 1915 as wagons and coaches are being used. Automobiles were not allowed in the park until August 1, 1915. (Author's collection.)

In 1901, Harry Thurston came to Cody and taught school at Marquette. He became a forest service ranger the next year and in 1907 was named superintendent of Shoshone National Forest. He appears to be moving wood using a push sled. While he was a ranger, he helped build the Wapiti Ranger Station, roughly 30 miles from Cody. (American Heritage Center, University of Wyoming.)

In November 1907, Buffalo Bill and friends came to the TE Ranch for a hunt. "Camp Foley," a temporary name, was above the TE and was named for Cody's good friend, Col. Tom Foley. After the hunt, Cody commissioned artist and friend R. Farrington Elwell to produce an oil painting based on the photograph to commemorate the hunt. Cody is stretched out in front of the main tent. (BBHC, P.69.1944.)

Either prior to the hunt, or afterward, the hunters spent time at the TE. Col. Tom Foley (left) is talking with Buffalo Bill (center) and George T. Beck, manager of the Shoshone Irrigation Company. It was Beck who lived year-round in Cody and oversaw the growth and progress of the town for Col. W. F. Cody. (PCA, 95-75-55.)

In December 1908, while Ned Frost was hunting a bobcat on Cedar Mountain, his dogs chased it into a hole. Frost followed them and found himself in a cave. Subsequently, various groups explored the cave, including this one. In the first row, far right, is George Inman, and in the second row, far right, is R. C. Shultz. All others are unidentified. (PCA, 95-62.7.)

Regardless of what crop farmers planted, a good team of draft horses was needed. Most teams used for plowing were either made up of two horses or four horses. This team of six was used on the Shultz farm in the Sage Creek area east of Cody and may have been leveling and smoothing the field. (PCA, 02-18-35.)

Once the Shoshone Dam was built and the canal system was well established, farming and ranching became a little easier and more productive. R. J. Allen is seen here standing in the middle of his tall cornfield, barely visible, in the late 1910s. The exact location is not known. (Wyoming State Archives, State Parks and Cultural Resources.)

Alfalfa was another crop that was grown successfully around Cody. This field is located upriver from where the Marquette farms were before they were flooded. Originally the area was overseen by the Hammitt Ditch Company, but after several takeovers and name changes, it became the Lakeview Irrigation Company. (Wyoming State Archives, State Parks and Cultural Resources.)

A hay rake is bucking hay for stacking in a field south of the Shoshone River, which may have belonged to Frost and Richard. Across the river (not visible), in a secluded area high up on Jim Mountain in the Big Creek area, is the Circle H Ranch, owned by Budd and Chella Hall, which opened as a dude ranch about 1926. (PCA, 97-42-62.)

DR. LOUCET ARANDERSON. PRINCE OF monaco Capt. Bouree LOUIS TINY

The most famous hunt in the Cody area took place in September 1913 when A. A. Anderson, designer of Pahaska Tepee, invited Prince Albert of Monaco to visit. The hunt attracted national attention, and many other hunters inquired about joining the group, but Anderson kept the number small. "Camp Monaco," the site of the hunt, is northeast of Pahaska Tepee. In addition to Buffalo Bill and guide Fred Richard, the main principals were, from left to right, Dr. Loucet (the prince's doctor), Anderson, Prince Albert, Captain Bouree of the French army, and Louis Tinyre [sic] (the prince's artist, who designed and painted the sign on the tree). In 1988, the Yellowstone fires that burned at least 706,277 acres also damaged the tree. It was removed by helicopter in 1994, and a six-and-a-half-foot section is on display in the Buffalo Bill Historical Center. (PCA, 00-06-294.)

Charles "Spend-a-Million" Gates (son of John "Bet-a-Million" Gates), seen here shaking hands with Buffalo Bill, wanted to join the prince's hunt but arrived too late. Instead he hired Ned Frost to guide his group. Upon their return from the hunt and shortly after this scene, Gates was found dead in his private railroad car. The cause of his death was never determined. (BBHC, P.69.300.)

Josephine Goodman Thurston, daughter of Buffalo Bill's sister Julia Cody Goodman, opened Elephant Head Lodge in 1926 as a guest ranch. It is located near its namesake, a rock formation, on the North Fork. Not very big, the lodge could hold up to 20 guests. Josie was married to Harry Thurston, an early forest ranger. The lodge is still in existence today. (BBHC, P.5.1426.)

Another early dude ranch on the North Fork was Holm Lodge, now known as Crossed Sabres Ranch. It was built in 1907 by Tex Holm and was called Holm Lodge No. 1, while No. 2 and No. 3 were in Yellowstone. Tourists were brought from Cody to the lodge by Stanley Steamers, but the trips into the park were by horse and wagon. (Vaun Landgren collection.)

Goff Creek Lodge is named for the creek it is located on, which in turn is named for Johnny Goff, the outfitter and hunter. In 1906, the Goff family came to the North Fork from Gardner, Montana, just north of Yellowstone, by way of Jones Creek and settled here. The lodge began accepting guests under the ownership of Tex Kennedy, sometime in the late 1920s. (PCA, 99-37-15.)

The A2Z Ranch sits on the east side of the Southfork at the foot of Boulder Ridge, near Carter Mountain, and roughly 32 miles from Cody. It became a dude ranch about 1910 and was bought out by Valley Ranch in the late 1920s. It was a more casual dude ranch than Valley, but guests at the A2Z were allowed to use the tennis courts, the swimming pool, the recreation cabin, and enjoy the evening's entertainment at Valley. (PCA, 97-42.99.)

Valley Ranch had separate pack trips for boys and girls during the summer. This outfit (trail hands) is on a pack trip in the late 1920s. From left to right are (first row) unidentified, Ernie Reuger, Al Mensell, and unidentified; (second row) A. C. Newton, Van Jernberg, Evan Holman, two unidentified, and Red Powell. Newton was head guide for the girls pack trips for many years. (BBHC, P.69.2007.)

The Siggins family has lived on the Southfork since 1906 and owned several ranches. The Double L Bar Ranch was originally owned by Una Libby Kaufman, who sold it to Pricilla and artist Lawrence Tenney Stevens in 1939. Later, brothers and partners Don and Ray Siggins bought it, and Ray and his family lived there. Don and his family lived nearby on the Triangle X Ranch and are seen here in about 1950; from left to right are Ken, Stan, Don, Donna, and Roz. Ken bought the Double L Bar Ranch in 1970. (PCA, 02-18-31.)

The Colonel built a hunting lodge at Irma Lake, also named for his daughter, in the late 1890s. He sold it to William Rogers Coe in 1911. The Coe family vacationed here in the summertime, but it was a working cattle ranch year-round. The ranch is 8,000 feet in elevation and overlooks the Southfork valley with the Buffalo Bill Reservoir in the distance. (PCA, 91-48-59.)

Mary and Carl Ballinger had a ranch of about 80 acres on the Southfork. It started with just a small house, a chicken coop, and some dairy cows. The house, on the left of the photograph, never got much bigger even with the addition of three children, but the dairy barn and the rest of the ranch increased quite a bit. They had a Grade A dairy barn with about 35 milk cows, and Mary took the milk to town every day. They raised 300–400 laying hens as well as chickens, which they sold to the Burlington Inn at the Cody Depot, as did many other ranchers. The Ballingers raised peas as a cash crop and would often plant them in March. Carl loved the cows and ranching but didn't care much for the farming part. (Mary Ballinger collection.)

Trailing cattle from range to range is a common occurrence. This herd is on Hwy 120 north of Cody, heading to the Two Dot Ranch. In the distance is Heart Mountain, the most predominant geological feature in the immediate Cody area. It was named Heart Mountain by the Indians because they thought it resembled a buffalo's heart. (PCA, 00-06-250.)

After Carl Ballinger's dad died in 1953, he and Mary decided to sell the Southfork ranch. In February 1954, they moved to the Stonebridge log house on the south side of the North Fork and had a 350-cow permit on Trout Creek. They made a great team as Carl worked the cattle and Mary kept the books. They loved having their grandchildren visit, and each one got a nine-mile trip to the cow camp the summer after their fifth birthday. (Mary Ballinger collection.)

Four

"RODEO CAPITAL OF THE WORLD"

The Cody Stampede is a three-day National Professional Rodeo–sanctioned rodeo that takes place annually over the Fourth of July. Additionally, every summer night during the months of June through August, there is a Cody Nite Rodeo. With that amount of rodeo during each summer, Cody is entitled to call itself the "Rodeo Capital of the World." Occasionally a trick buffalo gets into the act. (PCA, 91-02-110.)

It seems that a rodeo of some sort has almost always been a part of Cody's Fourth of July celebration going back to the earliest days. In 1907, Tom Trimmer competed in a stakes race on the grounds that were located where the Buffalo Bill Historical Center is today. The brick school in the background is southeast of the rodeo grounds. (PCA, 00-06-91.)

Bucking Broncho.
Cody. Wyo.
July 4-07

The name of the bucking broncho is Star, and "All the best riders tried him" in 1907, according to the notation written around the border of this photograph. The original owner of the photograph was Brownie Newton, and he went on to say, "Star was never ridden in Cody." (BBHC, P.69.1713.)

This cowboy has roped his steer, and his horse is backing up to show that the rope is secured tightly. There appears to be a very good crowd of people in buggies and in coaches and riders on horseback for this rodeo. Interestingly, several ropes have been left lying around in the arena and are visible in the foreground. (BBHC, P.69.2017.)

Two local cowboys, Blocker Dodge and Oscar Thompson, are having a hard time getting this horse under control in 1908. During the off-season, Buffalo Bill would be looking for new stock from local ranches for the Wild West and would hold tryouts on the vacant lot west of the Irma, where the hotel parking lot is now. (BBHC, P.69.1699.)

Good bucking horses keep coming back, and in 1908 Star was still bucking cowboys off. It didn't matter who you were; he didn't play favorites. Here is future Hollywood star Tim McCoy trying his best to stay on but not succeeding. McCoy eventually had his own Wild West show in 1936. (BBHC, P.5.1434.)

Holding the tryouts next to the Irma gave everyone in town a chance to watch. Francis Hayden, son of Charles Hayden, the surveyor who laid out the town of Cody in 1896, tells of watching these tryouts from the living room of his house with his brother when they were young boys and how much they enjoyed it. George Gardner is on "Blue Dog." (BBHC, P.5.7.)

The Fourth of July parade in 1909 was just as big an event as the rodeo, maybe even bigger. The parade took place before the rodeo, and the cowboys and cowgirls rode in it. The route took them along Sheridan Avenue just as it does today, although then the parade headed west instead of east. (BBHC, P.69.847.)

In 1909, fifteen-year-old Carly Downing enters the bucking horse contest at the Fourth of July Stampede and wins a prize. Both Carly and his brother George later appeared in Buffalo Bill's Wild West for a couple of years. In 1939, Carly started his nightly Pup Rodeo for young amateur cowboys. It was soon known as the Cody Nite Rodeo. (BBHC, P.69.1706.)

Bronc riding seems to have been the most popular event in those early years. It, calf roping, and bulldogging (now known as steer wrestling) are three rodeo events that are fairly similar to events in today's rodeo. There still are no corrals around the rodeo grounds, but people park their cars there, and they act as some sort of boundary. Photo taken by Finley Goodman in 1910. (BBHC, P.69.2185.)

Sheridan Ave. Cody. Wyo.

The main intersection of Cody was Sheridan Avenue and Twelfth Street (formerly Fourth Street) in 1913. Its nickname is the "4 Corners," and the front doors of the four corner businesses all face the center of the intersection. The Irma is out of the photograph on the right, and the identity of the cowboy is unknown. (BBHC, P.5.1463.)

Cody's Fourth of July celebrations became bigger as the years went on, attracting more participants from both northern Wyoming and southern Montana each year. The Cody Cowboy Band is seen just behind the first group of cowboys and was patterned after the Wild West Cowboy Band. Buffalo Bill paid for the instruments and the uniforms. (Wyoming State Archives, State Parks and Cultural Resources.)

Each winter's snowfall kept the roads into Yellowstone National Park closed until June and sometimes even later in the summer. Therefore, the opening of the East Entrance to the park was cause for great celebration. Clarence Williams, a longtime resident of the town and also a former cowboy with Buffalo Bill's Wild West, decided to hold a rodeo in 1919 to celebrate "Entrance Day," as it was called. This stagecoach went to Billings to promote the event. (PCA, 00-66-15.)

Caroline Lockhart was a newspaper woman who came to Cody in 1904. She had worked on papers in Boston and Philadelphia and became known as "Suzette" at the latter. She wrote several books, some of which became best sellers; some were also made into movies, including the *Fighting Shepardess*. Her second novel was the *Lady Doc*, which was a thinly disguised account of contemporary Cody society and caused the town to take sides between Dr. Frances Lane and Lockhart. By 1920, she was editor of the *Cody Enterprise* and was instrumental in starting the Fourth of July Stampede celebration. She was the first president of the board of directors, and to this day, she is the only woman who has served on that board. (PCA, 86-034–086.)

Floyd Noble's first day.

Cody Stampede, 1921.

Floyd Noble was a local cowboy who performed at the Cody Stampede for many years. However, this was his first day and one he probably remembered for many years as the horse gave him quite a good tumble. The rodeo grounds were then located on the east side of Cody, around the present-day Circle Drive area and near the road to the town of Powell. (PCA, 86-016-005.)

ROMAN STANDING RACE CODY STAMPEDE, (DOUBLEDAY)

One of the events at the Cody Stampede was the Roman Standing race, where riders stood on two horses and raced around the track. The new Cody Stampede grounds, located where the county fairgrounds had been, were a big improvement over the first ones, and while not all of the seats were under cover, the majority was. The stands faced east, which provided some shelter from the afternoon sun, which is when the rodeo was held. (PCA, 86-016-006.)

Nick Knight is seen riding Snakes at the Cody Stampede. Knight was a local Cody cowboy who became a world champion saddle bronc rider. He earned that title at Cheyenne Frontier Days in 1938 and was awarded a Powder River saddle as a prize. He was later inducted into the National Cowboy Hall of Fame. (BBHC, P.69.681.)

It is an honor to lead the Cody Stampede parade and to carry the American flags, which for many years A. C. Newton (left) and Dave Good did. The parade route is now longer and starts near the original Buffalo Bill Museum at City Park, moving east. A. C. Newton was an early owner of Trail Creek Ranch, and Dave Good was the manager of Caroline Lockhart's ranch. (PCA, 99-37.7.)

In 1946, the Cody Stampede grounds moved again. This time, they relocated to the top of the hill where the post office and the Park County Complex are today. The street is appropriately named Stampede Avenue. The covered area near the bottom of the photograph is where the broncs and the steers are released from the shoots into the arena. (PCA, 00-06-214.)

The Cody Stampede parade, held on the Fourth of July, has become the largest and most popular in Wyoming. Every politician who holds an office, whether it is local, county, state, or national, wants to ride in the parade if possible, especially if it is an election year. In 1986, Dick Cheney was Wyoming's only congressman. Here he is seen with his daughter Mary (left), his wife, Lynne (center, hidden), and daughter Elizabeth. (PCA, 91-02-144.)

Another annual participant in the parade is Uncle Sam. Dennis Haugan first walked in the parade in 1976 to mark the bicentennial of the country. This was his 10th year, and he still walks in the parade today. Vehicles used to be allowed to park along the curbs, which reduced the visibility of the crowd, but no longer. (PCA, 91-02-148.)

During 1996, a year-long celebration took place in Cody to commemorate the town's centennial. A reenactment of Buffalo Bill's Wild West was held at the stampede grounds during the weekend of June 15 and 16 with one daily performance. Ike Sankey, local rodeo stock contractor, headed the committee in charge of the production. "Buffalo Bill" and "Native Americans" are shown during the Grand Entry. (Author's collection.)

Five

THE MATURING TOWN

4534. Airplane View, Cody, Wyoming

After World War I, the town of Cody began to grow. The town government realized that more people required more services, better roads and bridges, and new construction in general. This mid-1920s aerial of Cody looking east shows many new buildings, including a school, and almost as many trees. (Wyoming State Archives, State Parks and Cultural Resources.)

Celeste Lawson, wife of telegrapher Leslie Lawson, is shown in the telegraph office on June 27, 1919. The office was located on Twelfth Street across from the east porch of the Irma Hotel, and it became affiliated with Western Union in 1923. Celeste became the county school superintendent in the late 1920s. The Lawsons' son Jim graduated from Cody High School in 1937 and went on to become an outstanding organist and carillonneur (bell ringer) at the Riverside Church in New York City and the Crystal Cathedral in California. (Nancy Trimmer Wulfing Collection.)

The first garage in Cody was owned by Glen Newton and Dudley Watkin, who named it the Park Garage. Lloyd Buchanan, third from the left, then purchased and renamed it the Cody Garage. It was a fixture at this location, across the street from the Irma Hotel's vacant lot on Sheridan Avenue, for many years. (American Heritage Center, University of Wyoming.)

Vaun Landgren is walking on a hanging bridge that crossed the Shoshone River about five miles west of Cody. It was a temporary bridge built for the construction workers so they could get back and forth across the river while they were building the Hayden Arch Bridge. (Vaun Landgren collection.)

The Hayden Arch Bridge was completed in the early 1920s and crosses the Shoshone River before the road enters the steeper part of the canyon. The road has been straightened out, and it no longer crosses the river at this point. A new bridge was built a little farther west and is called the Shoshone River Bridge. The Hayden Arch Bridge is still there, and the road allows access to the river. (Vaun Landgren collection.)

With William F. Cody's death on January 10, 1917, the people of Wyoming and Cody wanted to honor his memory. A national fund-raising campaign was started, which included the Boy Scouts collecting buffalo nickels for Buffalo Bill. Gertrude Vanderbilt Whitney was commissioned to produce a sculpture, and *Buffalo Bill—The Scout* was dedicated on July 4, 1924. The Buffalo Bill Museum, also established to honor his memory, opened three years later to the day. (BBHC, Jack Richard Collection, P.89.279.)

Many celebrities attended the dedication of the Buffalo Bill Museum on July 4, 1927, including former Wild West performers, Sen. John Kendrick of Wyoming, and Cody family members from around the country. Standing at the entrance to the museum is an extra-special guest, Alice Roosevelt Longworth, daughter of Pres. Theodore Roosevelt. The museum was modeled after Buffalo Bill's TE Ranch. (BBHC, P.6.833.)

Pres. Calvin Coolidge (center) visited Cody a month later to tour the Buffalo Bill Museum. Standing on the left is Mary Jester Allen, niece of Buffalo Bill, and the director and the curator of the museum. On the right is Jane Garlow, daughter of Irma Cody Garlow and Buffalo Bill's granddaughter. When President Coolidge left the museum, he went through the west door, thereafter known as the "Coolidge Door." (BBHC, P5.1499.)

Whether it was the effect of President Coolidge's visit or not, Jakie Schwoob, owner of Cody Trading Company, has a Coolidge sticker in his car window. The large, two-story house behind him was first used by the employees of the Irma Hotel and later by Louisa Cody, wife of Col. W. F. Cody, and their grandchildren after the death of their parents, Irma and Fred Garlow, from the Spanish influenza in October 1918. (PCA, 99-37.193.)

George T. Beck owned the first light plant, built in 1904 just above the Depot Bridge on the south side of the Shoshone River. With the construction of the dam, the Reclamation Service built a new power plant just below the dam on the north side of the Shoshone River. (Vaun Landgren collection.)

George T. Beck (left) and Mike Russell of Deadwood, South Dakota, good friends of Buffalo Bill's, are standing on Beck's porch. After buying his ranch on the Southfork in 1895, Cody bought horses and cattle from Russell. The herds were already branded with TE, so he decided to keep the brand and name the ranch after the brand. TE may stand for Trail's End, but that is uncertain. (PCA, 95-75-104.)

This is the new Cody Trading Company, which was rebuilt at the same location at the corner of Thirteenth Street and Sheridan Avenue after the fire in 1913. By the late 1920s, the inventory the store carried was enormous and owner Jakie Schwoob's motto was "We Sell Everything." (PCA, 99-37-89.)

Dave Jones came to Cody in 1907 and opened a men's clothing store that carried top-of-the-line merchandise, including Hart Schnaffer and Marx, Stetson Hats, and Florsheim Shoes. His motto was "Buy it of Dave Jones" which was seen all over the region on signs and even as far away as France during World War I. Vaun Landgren is standing next to one of his billboards not too far from Cody. (Vaun Landgren collection.)

Val Kirk (left) is congratulating Glenn Nielson on his purchase of Husky Oil in 1938. The company headquarters and the refinery were north of town near the Cody Depot. When the rodeo grounds moved from Stampede Avenue to the west side of town in 1976, Husky built their headquarters there. It is now the Park County Complex, and the Cody branch of the Park County Library will occupy part of the building in 2008. (BBHC, Jack Richard Collection, P.89.1385.)

This was the first Husky gas station in Cody, located at the corner of Sheridan Avenue and Sixteenth Street. It was a full-service facility and was owned directly by the company. In 1976, Husky's refinery was bought out by a Canadian firm, but this station remained a Husky station at least until 1982. There is still a station at this corner, but gas has not been sold here since 2006. (Wyoming State Archives, State Parks and Cultural Resources.)

This is Sheridan Avenue, known locally as "Main Street," looking west toward Rattlesnake Mountain in 1939. Wolfville, the local dance hall, is on the left. It was the scene of the annual Fourth of July evening festivities, which included dancing and gambling. Advertisements promoted the evening as "Our night to howl." It was used year-round as well until it burned down in July 1940. (BBHC, P.5.1470.)

Ethel Strayer James is standing in front of the Sanidary Store located on the north side of Sheridan Avenue near the Fourteenth Street corner. Ethel taught school in the community of Clark, north of Cody, when she first came to this area in 1940 and worked at the Sanidary Store in the summers. She and Frank James were married in 1946 and sold the store to J. C. and Martha Morris in 1948. (Fran Swope collection.)

In 1946, an extra-special birthday celebration was held at the Irma in honor of Buffalo Bill's 100th birthday. The Buffalo Bill Birthday Ball is held annually on the Saturday nearest to his birthday, February 26. Standing on the front porch of the Irma are, from left to right, unidentified, Harry Thurston, four unidentified, Clarence Williams as Wild Bill Hickok, Mary Jester Allen, three unidentified, Finley Goodman as Buffalo Bill, Josie Thurston, unidentified, and Larry Larom as Lt. Col. George Armstrong Custer. (BBHC, P.5.1588.)

The Budweiser Clydesdales periodically come to Cody and other towns in the Big Horn Basin to take part in parades and celebrations. They are usually sponsored by an individual business or two to help defray expenses. About 1952, it appears that they were sponsored by Norris Chevrolet (Greybull) before coming to Cody. Standing alongside them, from left to right, are Cody residents: Fran James (Swope), Ethel Strayer James, unidentified, Frank James Jr., unidentified, and Frank James Sr. (Fran Swope collection.)

After selling the Sanidary Store in 1948, Frank and Ethel James bought Frenchy's Diamond Bar on Sheridan Avenue between Twelfth and Thirteenth Streets. In the 1950s, there was still a Wyoming law that a bar could not employ a female bartender. Since Frenchy's did employ one, they were taken to justice court on August 23, 1956, where they were found guilty and were fined $100 plus court costs. The prices for drinks on the list behind the bar range from 25¢ to 65¢. (Fran Swope Collection.)

This is the intersection of Sheridan Avenue and Thirteenth Street in about 1960, looking west toward Rattlesnake Mountain. At the far end of the street, barely visible, is *Buffalo Bill—The Scout*. When it was installed in 1924, sculptress Gertrude Vanderbilt Whitney made sure it was situated so that it is visible the entire length of Sheridan Avenue. (Wyoming State Archives, State Parks and Cultural Resources.)

One of the most devastating fires in Cody's history occurred on Sunday, May 19, 1974. A fire started in a shed behind the *Cody Enterprise* building on Thirteenth Street. It spread to the newspaper's roof, smoldered overnight, and by noon the next day, it was a full-blown fire. Volunteer fireman Bob Moore tried to rescue reporter Eric Olson, but they both died from smoke inhalation, though Moore lasted five days. Photographer Dewey Vanderhoff escaped, and the arsonist confessed three and a half years later. (PCA, 02-38-358.)

In 1976, the Winchester gun collection was permanently loaned to the Buffalo Bill Historical Center by Olin Corporation. Part of it was put on display and opened to the public on the Fourth of July. At the ceremony, from left to right, are Rev. R. Nelson Buswell, Dr. Harold McCracken, John Wayne, William Tally, Cliff Hanson, Peg Coe, Peter Hassrick, and (at podium) Curt Gowdy. Wayne was the grand marshal of the Stampede Parade that year. (Wyoming State Archives, State Parks and Cultural Resources.)

Six

HISTORIC HOMES
AND BUILDINGS

Daisy Sorrenson Beck and George T. Beck built their house facing Eleventh Street in about 1909. Daisy Beck taught school in Marquette when she first came to Cody before becoming the secretary for the Shoshone Irrigation Company and working for George Beck. Their house became the social center of the town, and many of the residents still can describe parties they attended at the Becks' lovely home. Unfortunately it was torn down in 1966 to make way for the Manor, an apartment complex for senior citizens. (PCA, 86-001-011.)

The TE Ranch was purchased by Buffalo Bill, standing in front of the flagpole, from Bob Burns in 1895. Located roughly 24 miles southwest of the town of Cody, the TE was Buffalo Bill's favorite place to stay when he came home at the end of the Wild West season. Over the years, he added rooms to this log house. His land holdings eventually came close to 8,000 grazing acres, and his herd of cattle totaled 1,000. (BBHC, P.69.287.)

The original Bobcat Ranch was was located on Buffalo Bill's TE Ranch. It was used by May Cody Decker and her husband, Louis Decker, who also managed the Irma Hotel for Col. W. F. Cody. Standing in front of the ranch house, from left to right, are Roy Myres, Rella Myres, and May Decker. Later it was a dude ranch under the management of Carly Downing, former Wild West cowboy and rodeo performer. (BBHC, P.6.437.)

It did not take long for the Irma Hotel to attract guests and townspeople alike. From its opening on November 18, 1902, until today, it has always been the most prominent building in town. "Meet me at the Irma," or words to that effect, have been part of the town's rhetoric since its early days. This photograph was taken not too long after the hotel opened. Buffalo Bill is seen next to the wooden sidewalk in the center of the photograph. (BBHC, P.6.546.3.)

The interior of the Irma was elegantly decorated, as the dining room, now called the Governor's Room, shows. Julia Cody Goodman is seated at the head of the first table on the left but the others are unidentified. The painting on the left wall is the famous one by French artist Rosa Bonheur, a great admirer of Buffalo Bill's, who painted it when the Wild West was in Paris in 1889. It is now owned by the historical center. (BBHC, P6.861.)

John E. Kearns, third mayor of Cody from 1903 to 1904, built this house on Alger Avenue in 1902. He sold it for $4,000 to Sarah and William Hogg, sheep ranchers from Meeteetse, in 1909. It is this two-story home that is visible in most of the photographs taken from the Seventeenth Street hill, also known as the Greybull Hill. It has been owned by Carol and Ron Hill since 1969. (Author's collection.)

The Reuben C. Hargraves house is on the corner of Eleventh Street and Rumsey Avenue, across the street from where the Beck house was, and still stands today. Hargraves is probably the man holding the horse, as his hobby was raising harness race horses. The other three people are unidentified. Hargraves was a sheep rancher whose ranch was north of Cody, but as was common for sheep ranchers, his main home was in town. (PCA, 95-180-176.)

This house, built in 1904 or 1905, was located behind the Irma on Beck Avenue and was used by the employees of the hotel. It had two separate staircases leading to the upstairs, one for the women and one for the men. Later, Buffalo Bill's wife, Louisa, and their grandchildren lived here. In 1974, it was moved to Robertson Street just off of the Southfork Road and was made into a bed-and-breakfast. (Author's collection.)

Jakie Schwoob was a Wyoming state senator from 1905 to 1913 and built this house on the northwest corner of Fourteenth Street and Rumsey Avenue. Many years later, when it was owned by the Hindman family, it burned down. In 1913, when Schwoob was president of the Wyoming state senate, licensing of vehicles was made mandatory. He obtained license plate No. 1 for the entire state, which he kept even after the legislature went to a county numbering system in 1929. (Wyoming State Archives, State Parks and Cultural Resources.)

Pahaska Tepee is Buffalo Bill's hunting lodge on the North Fork, located about 50 miles from Cody. The Colonel picked out the site himself, blazing trees with an ax to mark the location. This is the area that he liked and where he brought hunting parties. Pahaska was completed in 1904, just three miles from the park. The road from Cody to Yellowstone was completed in 1903, the same year the entrance to Yellowstone was opened. (BBHC, P.6.446.)

This house is located on the Shoshone River below the Highway 120 (Depot) Bridge, to the right. It was built around 1908 by Florence Fell Oskins, mother of local Cody artist Olive Fell and her brother Bill. Oskins also built a green house there in which she grew flowers for her flower shop. Olive later owned the Four Bear Ranch on the North Fork and became well known for her drawings of bear cubs. Bill was a lawyer who later took over his mother's flower shop. (PCA, 86-021-018.)

The Cody Carnegie Library, shown here, was built in 1916 and was the second library at this site. The first library was built in 1906 with monies raised by the Women's Club of Cody. It was a very small one-room building that was soon outgrown. By 1963, the Carnegie Library was also too small and was torn down, much to the disappointment of many of the townspeople who hoped it could be saved somehow. It was replaced by the present library, which, in the fall of 2008, will relocate to the Park County Complex on Stampede Avenue. The Cody Library is the main branch of the Park County Library System, which includes the towns of Powell and Meeteetse. (BBHC, P.69.1355.)

In 1909, the Wyoming Legislature authorized the separation of a new county from Big Horn County. Cody was named the county seat of Park County and the next year began organizing and holding elections. By 1911, Park County was up and running, but the building housing the county offices was too small. The following year, construction began on a new building located on land given by Col. W. F. Cody on Sheridan Avenue. (PCA, 86.8-9.)

Construction began on the L. R. Ewart house in 1910 and was finished in 1912. It is on the corner of Tenth Street and Bleistein Avenue. Sitting on the front steps are, from left to right, Dorothy, Erwin, and Keene Ewart, children of Louis and Gertrude, about 1918. Louis, or "L. R." as he preferred to be called, was president of the First National Bank of Cody and was active in the Cody Club. He was elected to the Wyoming Legislature for three terms, serving as Speaker of the House in his last term in 1920–1921. (John Kappler collection.)

4545. Burlington Cody Inn, Cody, Wyoming

The Burlington Inn, also known as the Cody Inn, was built by the Burlington Railroad in the early 1920s near the depot. It had over 90 rooms with a dining room that could seat between 400 and 500 people. It was considered *the* place to go for special dinners by area residents. The parking lot of the inn was filled daily with upward of 50 buses waiting for the tourists to arrive on the *Buffalo Bill Special.* (Author's collection.)

William F. Cody lived in this home in Le Claire, Iowa, for about four years. In 1933, the home was offered to the Buffalo Bill Museum by the Burlington Railroad. It was shipped here in pieces and reassembled near the Cody Depot. In 1949, it was moved to the grounds of the museum in City Park, and then again in 1972 to the historical center. Its last move was in 2003 when it was moved 100 yards into Greever Garden at the center. (Fran Swope collection.)

Ida and Dave Jones and their daughter Eugenia came to Cody in 1904. Dave went to work for H. P. Arnold first and then L. L. Newton before opening his own store a year later. They built this house on Rumsey Avenue next to the Hargrave house in 1926. Originally their property belonged to the Hargraves and their carriage house was on the Jones property. (Author's collection.)

Coe Lodge on the Southfork is located on Irma Lake, named by Col. W. F. Cody for his daughter. Originally it was a hunting camp with a barn, built as early as 1897, and a cabin. In 1911, Cody sold it to W. R. Coe, who built a phenomenal lodge and cabin that became the family summer home. The original lodge was destroyed by fire in 1938 but was rebuilt by 1941, as seen in this photograph. (PCA, 91-48-59.)

Mary Jester Allen, director and curator of the Buffalo Bill Museum, sent out this Christmas card in 1941. The museum had been here for almost 15 years by this time, and the planting was well established. The mound covered with snow just to the left of the small wagon under the roof of the museum is a pile of elk horns, a common Wyoming sight. (Vaun Landgren collection.)

The following year, Mary Jester Allen's Christmas card was a photograph of herself taken at her home on Rumsey Avenue. The home is about a block from the former museum and is still there. Allen was the director and curator until she died in 1960, though she was in poor health during her last years. Her daughter, Helen Cody Allan, who had been married to a man who spelled his name Allan, acted in her place until 1961. (Vaun Landgren collection.)

Oilman Paul Stock was the largest individual shareholder of Texaco stock in 1944. One year later, he began construction of this house overlooking the Shoshone River for his second wife, Bertha, who died shortly after it was completed in 1946. The interior totals 6,700 square feet with original furnishings by Cody furniture maker Thomas Molesworth and a mural painted by local artist Ed Grigware. Stock was mayor of Cody from 1940 to 1944 and again from 1946 to 1948. The Paul Stock Foundation has contributed money and land to numerous projects throughout the town for over 40 years. The house was left to the BBHC in 1985 after the death of his third wife, Eloise. It was listed on the National Register of Historic Places (NRHP) on January 27, 2000. (Author's collection.)

This aerial is of Olive and Glenn Nielson's home on Skyline Drive. Built in 1947, it sits at the edge of the bench overlooking Sulphur Creek and the portion of the Yellowstone Highway known as the "West Cody Strip." The tennis court is no longer there, but the smaller house is and is used as a rental. The hay field in the foreground was their ranch land, which they donated to the city for the Olive-Glenn Golf and Country Club. (Margaret Ruth Bullock collection.)

Frank Lloyd Wright said that he wanted to build a house for Ruth and Quin Blair because he had never built a home in Wyoming. Built in 1951–1952, it is made of stone and wood to meld with its natural setting and is indicative of the direction that Wright's style took after World War II. It sits on 40 acres and is isolated from the highway now that the trees have grown up all around it. It was listed on the NRHP on September 27, 1991. (PCA, 95-33-1.)

Margaret "Peg" and Henry Coe began building this house in 1956 and finished it two years later. Nicknamed the Coe Mansion by some townspeople, it has seen many great events over the years. It has six bedrooms, seven baths, a swimming pool, and a six-car garage with a two-bedroom apartment above it. The Coes were married in 1943 and in 1946 bought Pahaska Tepee, which is still in the family. (PCA, 95-54-4.)

The house faces Rattlesnake Mountain to the west with the Southfork Hill (left) and Park Avenue in front. Upon Henry Coe's death in 1966, Peg was appointed to the historical center board of trustees to fill his position. She was elected chairman of the board in 1974, a position she held until she retired in 1997. This house was left to the center upon her death in November 2006. (Peg Coe collection.)

Seven

CHURCHES AND SCHOOLS

Construction of the First Presbyterian Church, located on the southwest corner of Beck Avenue and Eleventh Street, began in 1910 though the church had been organized since 1905. Rev. E. L. Anderson and probably the building committee are seen here. From left to right are (first row) Archie Brinkhorst, Dr. James Bradbury, Anderson, E. B. Rossiter, and Dr. F. Alsworth Waples; (second row) S. C. Parks Jr., Chas Parker, R. C. Hargraves, Fred Barnett, and Dave Jones. (Wyoming State Archives, State Parks and Cultural Resources.)

The Methodist church organized on January 18, 1902, and built this church on Beck Avenue and Fourteenth (then Sixth) Street. It was dedicated in the fall of that year, and Rev. E. P. Hughes was the first pastor. The congregation shortly outgrew this church, and a new one was built on Cody Avenue. This original church is now a bed-and-breakfast known as the Parson's Pillow. (PCA, 89-42-88.)

This is the second Methodist church, built in 1916 and dedicated on October 16 of that year. It sustained a fire in 1936 that destroyed most of the interior, but it was rebuilt by the next year. A new church was built on this site on the northeast corner of Beck Avenue and Fourteenth Street and was dedicated in 1962. (PCA, 00-06-94.)

This first Christ Episcopal Church is known affectionately as the "Poker Church" to this day. The starting funds to build it came from the winnings of a poker game held at Tom Purcell's saloon. Participants in the game were Col. W. F. Cody, George T. Beck, Tom Purcell, and two Meeteetse ranchers. When the pot reached $500, it was determined that it was too much for any one person to win and should be donated to the church of his choice. Beck chose the Episcopal church, which was built for $2,000 in 1902. (PCA, 89-23-5.)

The Christ Episcopal Church manse, built in 1911 by Rev. John Haight and his wife, hasn't changed much structurally. It was next door to the church, so when Reverend Haight was transferred later that same year, the church bought the house from him. It was used as the manse until a new church was built on Simpson Avenue and another house closer to the church was purchased in 1965. The Poker Church was moved to the grounds of the new church in June 1965. (Author's collection.)

These are some the people who attended the First Presbyterian Church in about 1917. Some of the children in the first row are Thruley Sorge, Maxine Baglin, Jeanette Siggins, Elizabeth Thurston, Merna Richards, Irene Norrell, and another Norrell. From left to right, the adults are (second row) Effie Edminster, Ethel Erickson, Clara Holm, and Marjorie Hayes; (third row) Gladys Erickson, Eugenia Jones, Elsie Ebert, Mildred Siggins, Electa Howe, Irene Spencer, Rev. Walter Gregg Pitkin, Julia Cody Goodman, Edith Holm, unidentified, Irene Wilson, G. A. Holm, and Algott Johnson; (fourth row) Flora and Guss Ebert, Frances Hill, Mildred Hayes, Luella Spencer, Van Howell, Olive Hansom, Fred McGee, Carl Cinnamon, Bill Smith, Joe Davis, Marian Ferris, Dave Jones, unidentified, Mrs. D. C. Smith, Minnie Williams, R. A. Edminster, and Natalie Siggins. (Wyoming State Archives, State Parks and Cultural Resources.)

In 1914–1915, these members of the First Presbyterian Church Sewing Circle earned money to help pay for the church. Pictured from left to right are the following: (lower steps) Kathryn Holland, Rachel Waples, ? Johnson, Elizabeth Holland, and Luella Harwell; (second row) Mildred Siggins, Mabel Ward, Dorothy Hiscock, Letha Fulton, Gladys Erickson, and Irene Spencer; (third row) Mildred Hays, Mildred Holm, Bessie Fulkerson, Mrs. F. C. Burnett, Jeanie Wilson, Mrs. Algott Johnson, Eugenia Jones, Dora Joslin, Camille Barnett, Dorothy Dayton, Francis Hall, and Ida Ward. (Wyoming State Archives, State Parks and Cultural Resources.)

The Presbyterian church is shown as it looked in 1936, just two years before the Hoopes Memorial Chapel was added to it. Maj. Ellis Hoopes served Park County as both its assessor and its sheriff at different times. Hoopes was a dedicated member of the church, and he left enough money to the church to build the chapel. (Len Pearson collection.)

St. Anthony's Catholic Church was built on Sheridan Avenue across the street from the Cody Public Library in 1915. The cost to build it was $2,300, of which $2,000 was donated by Nellie DeMaris, wife of Charles DeMaris. The church was built right next to their house (not visible). St. Anthony's was a mission church and did not have a resident pastor until 1944. In the background is the Park County Court House with the sheriff's house behind it. (PCA, 00-06-73.)

St. Anthony's bought land behind the current historical center in 1952, as the parish had outgrown the little church. The ground breaking took place in 1953, and it was dedicated the next year. A rectory was added in 1961. The little church stayed on Sheridan Avenue and became the County Extension Office but in 1985 was moved to Meeteetse and is now St. Theresa's. (PCA, 00-06-95.)

The First Presbyterian Church also outgrew its building, but there was no room to expand where they were. They bought land on Twenty-third Street, which was farmland, but initially only had enough money to construct the Sunday school building. By 1968, they were able to build the sanctuary, including the beautiful stained-glass windows from the original church and the chapel. The parlor window had been given by Buffalo Bill and his sisters Julia Goodman and Helen Wetmore in honor of their parents, Mary and Isaac Cody. (Author's collection.)

When Marquette was flooded, some families moved farther west to the Wapiti area on the North Fork, necessitating the building of a school. In 1910, school was held in this tent. Today the school has grades kindergarten through fifth grade, and they are part of Cody School District No. 6. From left to right are teacher June Hale Brundage, Vera Wagoner, Bill Leabold, Don Wagoner, Leonard Morris, and Herchall Green. (PCA.)

The first school in Cody built expressly as a school was the "Little Red School," which was built in 1904 and is seen here on the left. In 1909, the brick addition was built, more than doubling the capacity of the original school. All grades attended this school through high school. Francis Hayden, son of surveyor Charles Hayden, who laid out the town of Cody in 1896, is believed to be the small boy on the right edge of the photograph. (PCA, 00-06-227.)

Standing on the front steps of the Cody school are the students of the class of 1909 and their teachers. This was only the third class to graduate from the Cody school. The principal, E. B. Rossiter, is the man in front with the hat and bow tie. (PCA, 95-18-191.)

The class of 1917 is shown in front of the brick addition of the Cody school sometime in 1916. Among the almost 60 students pictured here, in the first row of those standing, are Milward Simpson (second from left) and Olive Fell (third from left). Simpson went on to be a state representative, governor of Wyoming, and then a U.S. senator. Fell became an artist known for her drawings of bear cubs, which are still very collectible today. (PCA, 86-021-019.)

When Marquette was flooded, Marquette School No. 1—the same school as seen previously—was moved to a new location not far from the reservoir. In 1926, May Norquist was the teacher, seen here standing just in front of the doorway. The students included Billy Capron, Darrel Way, Ruby Kinkade, Helmer Jensen, Dick Way, Wilbur Martin, Martin Gipe, Robert Way, Ralph Kinkade, Albert Miller, and Billy Stambaugh. (PCA.)

Another one-room school was on Monument Hill, an area northwest of Cody near Red Butte. Horseback was the best way for many rural students to get to school. In 1928–1929, the teacher was Clytie Fuson (not pictured) and the students were, from left to right, Lawrence Lundvall (back) and Dick Thompson; Victor Redding (back) and Betty Thompson; Mary Jensen (back) and Ellen Jensen; and Margaret Thompson (back) and John Jensen. (PCA.)

This is the Lower Sage Creek School, located east of Cody, in 1931. The teacher is Elsie Jensen and her students are, from left to right, Jean Hogan, Hazel Ebert (McJunkin), Leola Hogan (McMillan), Kirby Horner, and Ted Ebert. Elsie and the Jensens in the photograph above are all siblings. (PCA, 86-14-24.)

The Cody High School orchestra for 1936 is seen here. From left to right are (first row) Bert Siddle, two unidentified, Ester Johansson, two unidentified, Jean Bates, and music teacher Merle Prugh; (second row) all unidentified except far right, Dick Shaw; (third row) Billy Bosler, Bob Holm, Jim Lawson, two unidentified, Paul Smith, Geraldine Jones, and Glen Jobe. Others pictured are Ethel Edwards (violin), Marie Baier (violin), Harold Stump (drums), Allene Newton, ? McGee, and Ester Cowgill. (PCA, 00-02-12.)

The Hardpan school started in 1909, it is believed, on a ranch near Hardpan Creek about 20 miles from Cody. The building was then moved to the Shoemaker place at the head of the Lakeview Ditch on the Southfork and for a third time to the south end of the TE Ranch bridge. The school remained in use until 1963. (PCA, 00-6-304.)

Cody High School, which opened in 1922, has always offered agricultural classes. This group is the Agricultural III class for the school year 1943–1944. From left to right are (first row) Wayne Newell, Earl Martin, Martin Zinn, and Walter Nelson; (second row) Scott Taggart, Millard Meredith, Bert Schultz, Keith Kinkade, Bob English, Bill English, and Byron Wallace. (PCA, 01-35-9.)

The 1949 Cody High basketball team played their home games in Cody Auditorium on Beck Avenue. It was built by the city in 1942 on the site of the old Keystone Barn and leased to the high school beginning in 1946. From left to right are (first row) Bill Chambers, John Warner, Louis ("Jr.") Kousoulos, coach Glen Daniels, Charlie Pease, Don Kurtz, and Stanley Miller; (second row) Hal Lee, Dan Webster, captain Alan Simpson (a future U.S. Senator), Bob Moore, and Bud Cathcart. (PCA, 95-46-2.)

Eight

PEOPLE AND PASTIMES

Picnics in Cody are interesting pastimes. The weather may be cold, or the wind may blow, and there still may be snow on the ground. In the 1920s, picnic tables and campgrounds were in the future. Nonetheless, everyone enjoyed picnics even if they did get dirt and grit in their food, courtesy of the wind. From left to right are Marjorie Ross, Marian Finch, and Dr. Frances Lane. (Vaun Landgren Collection.)

About a mile west of Cody on the Shoshone River are mineral hot springs, long a favorite place of both Indians and locals. Charles DeMaris came to this area in 1883 from Montana and settled at the springs, first building a cabin and corrals and later a hotel. He developed the area into a health spa, even bottling water from the springs to sell. When W. F. Cody saw the springs, he wanted to establish the town of Cody here, and he even went so far as to have the town platted on the south side of the river just downstream. The DeMaris Hot Springs, as the area is called, became a favorite place for swimming, picnicking, and sunbathing for all ages. Many young people learned how to swim here, taught by longtime sheriff Frank Blackburn, who gave free lessons early in the mornings. From bottom to top are the pool house, the original bath house, the hotel, and the garage. The area is now privately owned and not open to the public. (Vaun Landgren collection.)

Earl and Harry

A necessary activity during the winter was cutting ice from the frozen upper Shoshone River. First the ice was scored into three-foot squares and then cut with a saw. Large ice clamps or tongs were used to pick them up. Earl ? (left) and Harry Reuger are "putting up the ice" on November 20, 1924. (American Heritage Center, University of Wyoming.)

Once the ice blocks had been cut, they were then loaded onto a cutter-type sled hitched to a team of horses. Earl (left) and Harry lead the sled with the ice home, where it would be stored in icehouses under hay or sawdust for future use. Ice was cut several times during the winter, depending, of course, on how long the cold weather lasted. (American Heritage Center, University of Wyoming.)

Harry Reuger

Once the ice cutting was finished, the fun could begin. Harry Reuger managed to get in a little skiing before heading back. Near Pahaska Tepee are places for both downhill and cross-country skiing that have been used since the 1920s. Sleeping Giant, a downhill area, did not open until the early 1940s. Cody High School annually fields both downhill and Nordic teams that compete in Wyoming and Montana. (American Heritage Center, University of Wyoming.)

"Etta Feeley's girls," as they are identified, are out for an afternoon horseback ride. Cody had a "red light" district in the early part of the 20th century near where Eastside School is today, and "Etta," real name Alice Leach, was a madam. The police allowed the houses to operate but would fine the madams whenever the town needed funds for new lighting or some other improvement project. (PCA, 02-15-28.)

For many years, Cody fielded a baseball team that played other teams in the Big Horn Basin, traveling by train to get to other towns. The ball field shared the Cody Stampede grounds with the rodeo during the years that the grounds were located where the historical center is now and then later at the Circle Drive area. Part of the Fourth of July activities included a baseball game. (PCA, 95-62-39.)

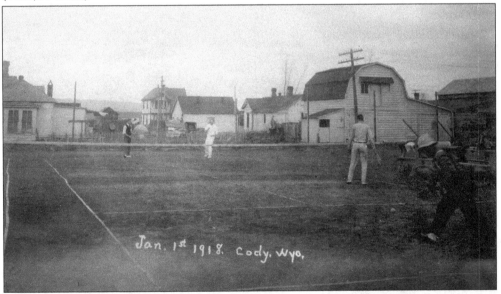

Tennis became popular in towns around the United States after World War I, and Cody was no exception. The players are dressed in the proper white attire and not winter clothes despite the fact that it is January 1, 1918. At one time, there was a court on the south side of Beck Avenue in the 1100 block, and this may be that court. (BBHC, P.69.1358.)

Buffalo Bill—The Scout makes a wonderful backdrop for a wedding. Gertrude Vanderbilt Whitney's statue was dedicated on July 4, 1924, just before Vaun and Stan Landgren were married here on June 14, 1925. They went to Yellowstone for their honeymoon, stopping at Holm Lodge on the North Fork along the way. Stan and Vaun are the two people standing on the far right. (Vaun Landgren collection.)

The Cody Golf Club began operation in 1928 near Newton Lake, north of Cody. The course was mostly dirt and sagebrush, but the players still enjoyed playing. The club moved east of Cody on the Greybull Highway in 1949 and changed its name to the Park County Country Club. In 1968, Olive and Glenn Nielson donated land on Skyline Drive, and the course was ready to play in 1970. (PCA, 01-52-6.)

The popular way to see Yellowstone was to ride in a yellow bus, called a "jammer." The name came from the nickname given to the drivers of the buses, who jammed the gears while driving. These buses traveled within the park only, showing tourists the sights and delivering them to hotels within the park. They have been refurbished and are being used once again. (Vaun Landgren collection.)

People aren't the only visitors to Pahaska. This bear has learned that there is more to humans than meets the eye, such as food. The interactions between bears and humans have changed over the years. It was considered fun to feed the bears, and tourists in Yellowstone used to bear watch at the open garage dumps. (Vaun Landgren collection.)

These two young gentlemen are George Landgren (left), age six, and Bob Landgren, age four. Their father, Stan, came to Cody in 1923 from Nebraska and was a member of the Cody Cowboy Band. He owned the Post Office Store from 1925, when he and Monte Jones bought it, until he retired in 1965. Bob still lives in Cody. (Vaun Landgren collection.)

Local artist Olive Fell is seen with her horse at her Four Bear Ranch, located on Jim Creek on the North Fork. With views such as this one, it is no wonder that Cody has become a gathering place for many artists over the years. Not only have painters gravitated here, but furniture makers, potters, sculptors, and other artisans have as well. (PCA, 86-021-021.)

Alice de Mauriac Hammond, daughter of Alice Bergen de Mauriac and Norman Parsons de Mauriac, is an interesting Cody personality. Her father bought a North Fork ranch on Trout Creek in 1916 as a summer place. N. P. increased the size of the ranch over the years and spent a lot of money doing it. Their only child, Alice, went to a private girls' school in Virginia and met her husband, Ben Hammond, on a European vacation. They lived at Trout Creek year-round, and Alice soon became known for her unusual ways, including promiscuity. Ben divorced her and moved back east, leaving Alice here with their two children. She received her doctorate in psychology, ran for Congress, spent lots of money, and had many boyfriends. When N. P. lost his fortune in the stock market in the late 1940s or 1950s and later died, the ranch was sold and Alice Hammond and her mother moved to town. As Hammond got older, her traffic tickets became more numerous and appearances in Cody stores dressed inappropriately became more common. (PCA, 86-37-170.)

An Easter egg hunt was given at the Beck house by their grandchildren on April 8, 1938. Sitting on the front porch steps are, from left to right, (first row) David Lofstrom, Nancy Trimmer, ? Lofstrom, Nancy Bane, Larry Slotta, and Jon Avent; (second row) Jim Slotta, Nebbe Johnson, Betty Jane Johnson, Alan Simpson, Buck Buchanan, Peter Simpson, and Dick Avent. The Beck grandchildren are Betty Jane and Nebbe. (Nancy Trimmer Wulfing Collection.)

Frank Houx and his unidentified young friend are sitting on the front porch of the Irma Hotel. Houx was Cody's first mayor in 1901–1902 and served again from 1906 to 1910; he was also governor of Wyoming from 1917 to 1919. In about 1939, Houx returned to Cody to live at the Irma, owned by his daughter Pearl Newell. He frequently was seen sitting here in his wheelchair if the weather was nice. (BBHC, P.69.1460.)

Sunday afternoons are great times for families to do things together, including playing Chinese checkers. Whether politics at the Simpson home was talked about during these games is not known, but more than likely it was. Pete (left), about 10 years old, was a state legislator and a vice president of the University of Wyoming in the 1980s. Their father, Milward (center), was a state representative, governor, and U.S. senator. Al, about nine, was a state senator and U.S. senator. (PCA, 91-48-9.)

The steep cliffs of the Absaroka Range of the Rocky Mountains offer adventurers different opportunities. Preparing to rock climb near the tunnels in Shoshone Canyon are, left to right: Terry Bartlett, Jerry Pyle, Kurt Waggoner, instructor Spike Beemer, Tom Brown, Bill Bickenhueser, and Bob Pyle. On the Southfork, ice climbing has become popular and attracts climbers from all over the country, and Buffalo Bill Reservoir offers windsurfers a real challenge. (BBHC, Jack Richard Collection, P.89.4013.)

On June 6, 1988, a 15¢ stamp was issued to honor Buffalo Bill Cody. The First Day of Issue ceremony was attended by, from left to right, Jack Rosenthal (Stamp Advisory Committee member), Jerry Lee (postmaster general, Central Division), Peg Coe (chairman of the BBHC board of trustees), Al Simpson (trustee), Gov. Mike Sullivan, Peter Hassrick (director, BBHC), Charles Kepler (trustee), Mayor Dorse Miller, and Fr. Charles Brady. (Author's collection.)

In 1996, as part of the town's centennial celebration, a balloon rally was held. The Wild West Balloon Fest has been an annual event held in August ever since. The balloon on the left is *Freedom*, owned by the Cody Balloon Club and flown by Ray Moss. *Kiss Again* is piloted by Greg Szymanski of Idaho. (Author's collection.)

On December 31, 1999, the town commemorated the start of a new century with a celebration called "Y2Kody." Activities throughout the day included a parade, a dance at the Buffalo Bill Historical Center, fireworks at midnight, and the dedication of a statue named the *Spirit of Cody* at the northeast corner of City Park on Sheridan Avenue. Sculpted by local artist Jeff Rudolph, it shows Buffalo Bill holding a young lad on his shoulders, gazing up at the sky, and waving the Colonel's Stetson. Eddie Three Rivers is shown blessing the statue. A time capsule was placed inside the base of the statue by the late Sen. Craig Thomas, a graduate of Cody High School. The capsule will be opened in 2049. (Author's collection.)

This is a label promoting the "Cody to Yellowstone Park Road" as the most scenic 70 miles in America. In later years, the mileage between Cody and Yellowstone decreased to 52 miles as the road was rerouted and straightened out, thereby eliminating most of the 26 crossings of the Shoshone River that were part of the adventure of traveling to Yellowstone. It is not known who printed the promotional label, though it may have been the Cody Club (Cody's chamber of commerce), but the phrase was coined by men's store owner Dave Jones. (Len Pearson collection.)

BIBLIOGRAPHY

Andren, Gladys. *Life Among the Ladies by the Lake*. Cody, WY: self-published, 1984.

Bartlett, Richard A. *From Cody to the World*. Cody, WY: Buffalo Bill Historical Center, 1992.

Barnhart, Bill. *The Northfork Trail*. Cody, WY: Elkhorn Publishing, 1982.

Churchill, Beryl. *Challenging the Canyon*. Cody, WY: Wordsworth, 2001.

Cook, Jeannie, et al. *Buffalo Bill's Town in the Rockies*. Virginia Beach, VA: Donning Company Publishers, 1996.

Frost, Dick. *Tracks, Trails, and Tails*. Cody, WY: self-published, 1984.

Hicks, Lucille P., ed. *The Park County Story*. Dallas, TX: Taylor Publishing Company, 1980.

Johansson-Murray, Ester. *A History of the Northfork of the Shoshone River*. Cody, WY: Lone Eagle Multi Media, 1996.

Kensel, W. Hudson. *Pahaska Tepee; Buffalo Bill's Old Hunting Lodge and Hotel, a History, 1901–1946*. Cody, WY: Buffalo Bill Historical Center, 1987.

Roberts, Phil, et al. *Wyoming Almanac*. 4th ed. rev. Laramie, WY: 1996.

Wasden, David. *From Beaver to Oil*. Cheyenne, WY: Pioneer Printing and Stationery Company, 1973.

Visit us at
arcadiapublishing.com

••